HAL•LEONARD®
VIOLIN PLAY-ALONG

AUDIO ACCESS INCLUDED

STAR WARS: THE FORCE AWAKENS
MUSIC FROM THE MOTION PICTURE SOUNDTRACK

T0066191

PLAYBACK+
Speed • Pitch • Balance • Loop

To access audio visit:
www.halleonard.com/mylibrary

Enter Code
6945-9353-1191-3844

ISBN 978-1-4950-6002-1

Jon Vriesacker, Violin

Audio Arrangements by Peter Deneff
Recorded and Produced by Jake Johnson
at Paradyme Productions

Utapau Music

DISTRIBUTED BY

7777 W. BLEUMOUND RD. P.O. BOX 13819 MILWAUKEE, WI 53213

Visit Hal Leonard Online at
www.halleonard.com

In Australia Contact:
Hal Leonard Australia Pty. Ltd.
4 Lentara Court
Cheltenham, Victoria, 3192 Australia
Email: ausadmin@halleonard.com.au

HAL•LEONARD®
VIOLIN PLAY-ALONG

AUDIO ACCESS INCLUDED

STAR WARS: THE FORCE AWAKENS
MUSIC FROM THE MOTION PICTURE SOUNDTRACK

CONTENTS

Main Title *and* The Attack on the Jakku Village

Music by John Williams

Moderately fast

mp

pp > *ppp*

Rey's Theme

Music by John Williams

molto rall.

a tempo

rit. e dim.

Finn's Confession

Music by John Williams

Han and Leia

Music by John Williams

March of the Resistance

Music by John Williams

Farewell *and* The Trip

Music by John Williams

mf *a tempo*

mf

f

mp

p

The Jedi Steps *and* Finale

Music by John Williams

Broadly

Quickly

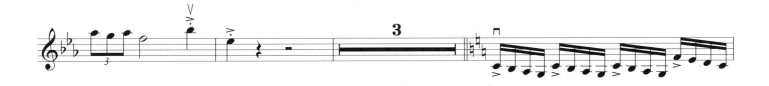

* cue notes optional

Torn Apart

Music by John Williams